Biographies of the Author and Illustrator

Ronald Paul Furstenau is a chemistry instructor at the United States Air Force Academy. He has done science and engineering outreach activities for kids and science teachers for 25 years. He loves to motivate kids to study science. He lives in Colorado Springs, Colorado with his wife Julie, who is a high school chemistry teacher. They both love to hike and bicycle.

Paige Anne Latendresse was born in North Carolina but currently lives in Colorado with her family. She is a proud 2011 graduate of Doherty High School in Colorado Springs, Colorado. She is attending college at Colorado State University to double major in Biology and Zoology. Her long term goal is to become a veterinarian with an emphasis in Zoo Medicine.

Dedication

This book is dedicated to my wife, Julie. She is the love of my life and the most caring person I have ever met. She is my hero.

Acknowledgments

The author would like to thank Dr. Ross Gresham in the Department of English and Fine Arts for reviewing the manuscript and testing it out on his kids. He made some superb suggestions for improving the story. The author would also like to thank Julie Imada from the Director of Research office at the USAF Academy for her help in turning the idea for this book into a reality. Finally, thanks goes out to Erik Landrum and Jessica Jones, who provided the design layout support for the book.

STEM Outreach at the United States Air Force Academy

The Air Force Academy supports a wide variety of STEM outreach activities for students in kindergarten through twelfth grade and their teachers. Thanks in large part to the volunteer efforts of faculty members and cadets, the Academy partners with regional nonprofit organizations and local industry groups to provide STEM educational opportunities for thousands of students across Colorado. The Academy also supports continuing educational opportunities and access to national resources for educators throughout the nation.

For more information about USAFA's STEM programs, please call 719-333-4195. Follow our K-12 STEM Mascot, Aurora Phd, on Facebook for the latest in STEM lesson plans, announcements about activities and other information. Follow her on Twitter at @msauroraphd.

For sale by the Superintendent of Documents, U.S. Government Printing Office
Internet: bookstore.gpo.gov Phone: toll free (866) 512-1800; DC area (202) 512-1800
Fax: (202) 512-2104 Mail: Stop IDCC, Washington, DC 20402-0001

ISBN 978-0-16-091707-3

Julie loved to go to school. She loved playing with her friends at recess.
Most of all, Julie loved to learn about new things.

Julie loved to ask questions in class. She especially liked math and science. She wanted to understand the world around her.

The other children in the class liked Julie.
They liked how she wasn't afraid to ask questions.
Julie's questions were always things the other
children wanted to know about, too.

7

Julie even liked to do homework! She loved to read. The more she read, the more she learned.

One evening after dinner, Julie was doing her homework for the next day. Tomorrow, it was her turn to start the class by sharing something with the class that she had learned from her homework. For some of her homework, she read about atoms and molecules in her science book. Julie thought this was really cool and couldn't wait to learn more. However, atoms and molecules were new to Julie and she wasn't sure what to tell the class.

But Julie was getting tired and it was time to go to bed. "Mom," said Julie, "I read about atoms and molecules in my science book tonight. Do you know anything about them?"

"Oh!" exclaimed Julie's mom. "You'll love learning about atoms and molecules. Everything is made out of different kinds of atoms and molecules. Atoms are the building blocks that make up molecules."

"Wow! Everything? Like my clothes and my books and my food?" asked Julie.

"Yes," said Julie's mom. "Including the air that you breathe and you! Now go to sleep so you'll be ready to learn more tomorrow."

Julie's mom made Julie think of even more questions. How big are atoms? What do atoms look like? How do atoms come together to form molecules?

But Julie was hungry. She hid some chocolate
candy bars in her room and decided to eat one before
going to sleep. After finishing the candy bar, she laid
her head on her pillow.

Not long after lying down, Julie heard a very faint noise coming from her pillow. It sounded like a voice, but she wasn't sure.

Julie remembered that putting a glass on a door can help magnify the sound from the other side. She kept a glass of water near her bed in case she got thirsty at night. Julie drank the water then put the glass on her pillow. Sure enough, Julie could hear a very soft voice. "Come closer!" the voice said. "Come closer? Come closer to what?" Julie thought. She couldn't see anything!

All of a sudden, Julie was inside the glass on her pillow! Everything in her room looked huge--the pillow, the glass, her clock . . . everything! "Come closer," repeated the voice.

Then, Julie could see the threads of cloth in her pillow.
The threads looked like huge logs that were criss-crossed.
"Come closer," the voice said again.

Now, everything seemed to disappear except a big, fuzzy ball.
"Come closer!" The voice was coming from the fuzzy ball.

Suddenly, a face appeared on the fuzzy ball. "Who are you?" asked Julie, in a shaky voice. Julie was a little frightened, but not too frightened. She had never seen a talking fuzzy ball before!

"I'm a carbon atom," said the smiling fuzzy ball.

"Where did you come from?" asked Julie.

"I came from the chocolate that was still around your mouth when you laid your head on your pillow. A tiny bit of chocolate fell on to your pillow case. I'm one of the atoms in that bit of chocolate. There are many millions of other atoms in that bit of chocolate, too," replied the fuzzy ball.

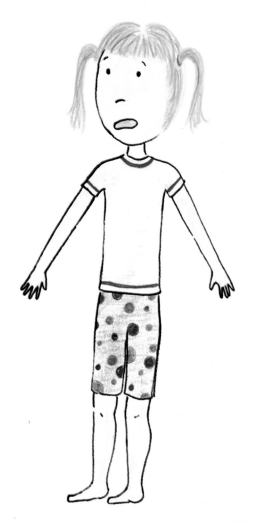

Julie's mom was right. Everything is made of atoms and molecules, even chocolate! Julie had many questions for the carbon atom. "My name is Julie. It's very nice to meet you. What makes you a carbon atom?" asked Julie.

"I have 6 protons," said the carbon atom, pointing to its center. "I also have 6 neutrons. They're with the protons in my nucleus. My nucleus is really small compared to the rest of me, so it's really hard for you to see."

"So the rest of you must be the electrons I was reading about in my homework," stated Julie. "You must have 6 electrons, the same as your number of protons."

"Yes," replied the carbon atom. "Depending on how you look at my electrons, they can behave like fast-moving little marbles or like waves in an ocean. They're pretty strange! My electrons hang around because they are attracted to the protons in my nucleus." Julie thought this was odd, but she kept asking more questions.

"So are you mostly electrons?" asked Julie. "Do your electrons make noise? Do they talk?"

"No, I'm mostly empty space," said the atom. "My size is determined by where my electrons can go, but almost all of my weight is in my nucleus, even though it is very tiny. My electrons are sort of like your hands and arms, so they don't make noise or talk. I can grab other atoms with my electrons. When I share my electrons with other atoms and they share their electrons with me, we call it a bond. It's the bond that holds us together to form a molecule."

"How big are you?" asked Julie.

"You had to become very small to see me," replied the atom. "If I and some other carbon atoms stood side-by-side on top of a penny, over 100 million of us would fit across the penny!"

"Do you have a name?" asked Julie.

"No," sighed the carbon atom.

"Would you like a name?" asked Julie.

"Oh, yes," said the carbon atom. "That would be very nice."

"How about Amelia?" said Julie. "My best friend in school has the name Amelia."

"That sounds wonderful!" the carbon atom said with a smile. "Amelia . . . I really like that name."

"Have you always been a carbon atom, Amelia?" asked Julie.

"Yes," said Amelia. "As long as I can remember. I've never been alone, though. For a long time, I teamed up with two oxygen atoms as part of a carbon dioxide molecule. We shared electrons, which kept us stuck together. Then, the leaves of a cocoa plant grabbed us and we became parts of new molecules in a cocoa bean. I lost the oxygen atoms. Then I ended up as part of a chocolate molecule in the candy bar that you ate."

"Do you miss the oxygen atoms?" asked Julie.

"A little," replied Amelia, "but I made lots of new friends in the chocolate molecule."

23

Suddenly, some of Amelia's friends from the chocolate molecule appeared. They were all very nice and wanted to say 'hi' to Julie.

Although Julie was enjoying her time with the atoms, Amelia could see that Julie was getting sleepy. "I think it's time for you to go back to your bedroom," said Amelia, with a smile.

The next thing she knew, Julie was awake in her bed, with her mom gently pushing on her shoulder. "Wake up, Julie!" said Julie's mom. "It's time to get ready for school!"

26

Julie was still a little groggy as she was putting on her clothes to go eat breakfast. "Amelia and the other atoms were just a dream," she thought. "But I learned a lot about them."

As she ate breakfast, Julie could not stop thinking about atoms and molecules. Her breakfast cereal was made out of different atoms and molecules. So was her orange juice, so was the glass that held the orange juice, and the air she was breathing . . . everything around her was made of atoms and molecules!

When Julie arrived at school, her teacher, Mrs. Smith, reminded Julie that it was her turn to start the class by describing something she had learned about in her homework from last night. Julie smiled. She knew exactly what she was going to talk about to the rest of the class!

Julie pulled a candy bar out of her backpack. "I learned a lot about candy last night," said Julie. "So that's what I'm going to talk about today."

"Cool!" exclaimed Jimmy, one of Julie's friends.

"This piece of candy is made out of lots of different things called molecules. It has molecules of chocolate and lots of other kinds of molecules," said Julie. "Each molecule is very tiny, so tiny that you can't see them. There are many, many millions of molecules in even a speck of this candy bar. Each molecule is made of even tinier things called atoms. The atoms have even tinier things in them called protons, neutrons, and electrons."

"That was wonderful, Julie!" said Mrs. Smith. "You learned a lot from doing your homework. Different molecules contain different combinations of elements," added Mrs. Smith, as she pointed to a chart called the *Periodic Table of the Elements* on the wall. "There are about a hundred different kinds of elements. Each element has a different name and symbol. The type of molecule depends on how the atoms of these elements are arranged."

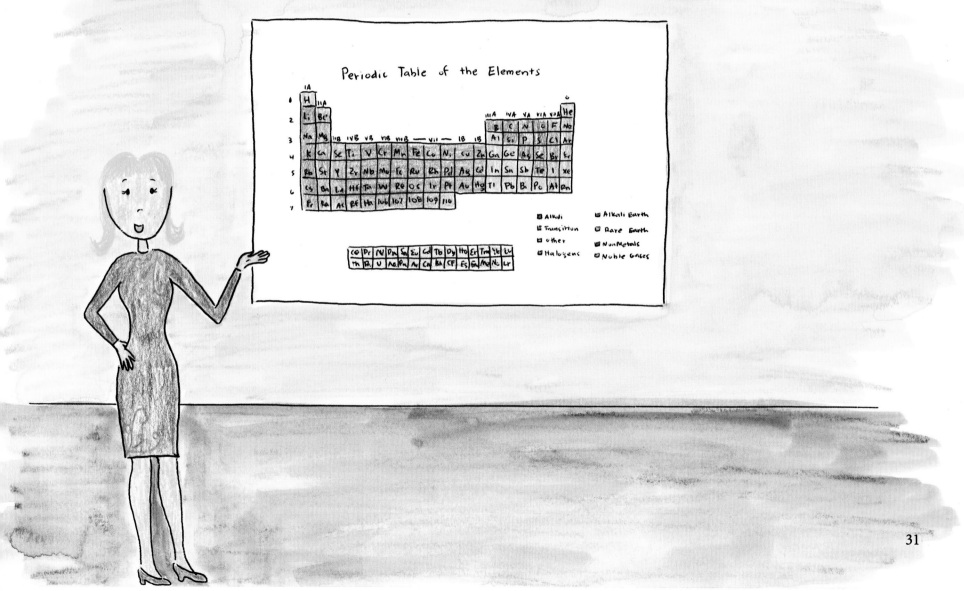

"When you eat a candy bar, your body switches the atoms around. When your body switches around the atoms, you can get energy to play at recess," explained Mrs. Smith. "Not only that, the atoms from the chocolate can then become part of your arm or your leg or your hair!"

Julie immediately thought of Amelia. Could Amelia be in my arm? My leg? My hair? Maybe Amelia is part of my ear that's helping me to hear Mrs. Smith right now!

"We're going to learn a lot about atoms and molecules in school this year," said Mrs. Smith. "We're going to do science experiments to help us understand how atoms and molecules behave. We're also going to make things by mixing different molecules together. We call this kind of science *chemistry*."

Julie learned a lot more about atoms and molecules in school that day. She discovered that she loved science and chemistry. She loved learning about what things were made out of and how things were put together. She had learned a lot about atoms and molecules from her mom and Amelia and Mrs. Smith. She was excited about learning even more. After all, everything is made of atoms and molecules!

Periodic Table of the Elements

	1A																	0
1	H	IIA											IIIA	IVA	VA	VIA	VIIA	He
2	Li	Be											B	C	N	O	F	Ne
3	Na	Mg	IIIB	IVB	VB	VIB	VIIB	— VIII —			IB	IIB	Al	Si	P	S	Cl	Ar
4	K	Ca	Sc	Ti	V	Cr	Mn	Fe	Co	Ni	Cu	Zn	Ga	Ge	As	Se	Br	Kr
5	Rb	Sr	Y	Zr	Nb	Mo	Tc	Ru	Rh	Pd	Ag	Cd	In	Sn	Sb	Te	I	Xe
6	Cs	Ba	La	Hf	Ta	W	Re	Os	Ir	Pt	Au	Hg	Tl	Pb	Bi	Po	At	Rn
7	Fr	Ra	Ac	Rf	Ha	106	107	108	109	110								

Ce	Pr	Nd	Pm	Sm	Eu	Gd	Tb	Dy	Ho	Er	Tm	Yb	Lu
Th	Pa	U	Np	Pu	Am	Cm	Bk	Cf	Es	Fm	Md	No	Lr

Alkali   Alkali Earth
Transition   Rare Earth
Other   NonMetals
Halogens   Noble Gases